looking for a sweetie
diya gitanjali mark

love poems / a coming of age story in no particular order

dedicated to
everyone who loves me
everyone who's spat in my mouth
everyone i've gotten sick
me, myself and i

small god

bring me
something that shines.
teeth in a smile
or else shining like tic tacs
in your outstretched palm.
brass bottle cap
$2 lip gloss
shard of sea glass.
don't you get it?

look me in the eye
when you speak
but don't stare, my love
don't linger.
my ancestors watch
from behind the veil of my corneas
they startle easily, these days.
you know how dark the nights get.
you know how hard it is
to breathe through
someone else's skin.

lean down
let me touch your shoulders
as i tell you
how they kept a small god
in a cat kennel.
how it thrashed and howled
clawed at the plastic

when i die
the mortician will hold my chin
reach into my mouth
peel back my purple lips
find a tiger's canines
in my gums.

outside
the crows
will be hopping
around the parking lot
telling jokes.
their laughter
climbs into the sky

 i understand now
i swear i do

haunted house

what if I kept you here / in my blue porcelain jewelry box / fed you droplets of
cheap wine / squeezed from a handkerchief / used you / pillow / scaffolding/
armrest / the lamp on my bedside table / can i make you light up?

 i'm sorry / i'm sorry i am an old house with creaky stairs / worn down paths in the
floors / women in nightgowns levitating in the hallways

you're too sweet for me / don't you know your way out?

autopsy

guts mealy as rotten fruit
bones of lead
oil spill saliva
my lover tells me
he wants to pack up the car
and drive out west.
my lover tells me
he wants to meet my dad.

my lover tells me
these things work out.

(years ago the doctors opened me up, scalpels and prying blue rubber fingers. under my
skin all they found was warm asphalt, the kind they fill potholes with.)

girl as
cherry sucker
dropped onto carpet
peeled away with a hair or two.

are you sure
you want to put
that in your mouth?

swan song

i can imagine sitting
on a wraparound porch

you're there with me
eighty something with
 a sinking face,
jowls that tremble when you talk
a gold watch
running backwards

look at us
hand in papery hand
sun spots on my temples
gray hair falling to my waist
my tattoos a bit shriveled
soft at the edges

say it again — wouldn't it be nice?

out west

what if you came out west
and i'd lived there all my life?

the end of the 19th century
the sky stretching in all directions
just like the desert, like God's eyes

what if i only ever wore frothy lace, layers of it
fucked strange men for gold pieces
railway workers and cowherds and husbands,
mechanical as the butcher and his cow,
the milkmaid and her pail.

sometimes when i go out in the daytime
people spit at my feet
hiss from doorways
murmur behind hands
i keep on walking
turn their curses to hymns.

we meet in the general store, anyhow.
i'm haggling with the clerk,
& there you are in your Sunday best
a starched shirt and clean hands
your mouth a soft *o*
my breathing turned slow
as a trickle of molasses

& what happens next?
a walk down to the ravine
your hand on my lower back
steadying me
you, giving me a chaste kiss goodnight
you, climbing the stairs to my room
your face hanging over mine
like the harvest moon
i've never seen anything like you.

is this alright?

you, gone with the next train
just like the rest
you, down on one knee
beaming up at me
wedding bells and a dozen empty pews.
what if you take me far away from here?
what if i spend my whole life
waiting at the window?

islands

in my dream
i stood on an island with flowers in my hair
and a woven skirt
around my waist
the trees were full of mist
air heavy with humidity
i was with someone.
not a brother but somehow closer
he lead me into the jungle
pushing branches out of my way,
clearing the path.
the trees grew darker and closer
not terrifying but
almost.
he held my hand,
said he had something to show me
it was just a little farther
but it felt like we were running away.

from what, I didn't know.
a monster with a thousand eyes
 the curse that our grandparents had brought upon us
running from whatever the future held.

we stumble out of the woods
but we are not the same

the boy dies within a month
drowned not far from shore
the riptide drags him away.
like the ocean wanted him for herself.

i follow a year later.
death by broken heart
they said,
not knowing it was a nasty strain of the yellow fever
that had overheated my system

and stopped my heart but
there wasn't a difference,
was there?
at least they got to bury me
deep beneath the warm rich earth
at least I wake up,
several centuries later beneath my Walmart blanket and cotton sheets.
wondering where I am.
wondering what it meant.

dreamgirl

i spent nights poking at my skin with needles,
examining, over critical
hacking at my hair with kitchen scissors
soaking it in bleach
letting my fingertips dissolve
anything to feel more
like myself.

i spent too long
under streetlights and in doorways,
standing up for someone who tried to make me feel small
tried to fold me up and stash me away for later.

i spent time with someone who told me
i needed to grow up
lose my sharp edges and my eating habits and my best friend
squeeze into the mold
she made for me.

i spent half a year
with the boy i'd dreamed of
not quite lucid and not quite awake
he feeds me disappointment by the spoonful,
bitter and stinging
and i wake up disoriented,
head aching
alone
what a beautiful thing
what a joke

the next is
friendship want and need
he teases joy out of me
like a long spool of thread,
silver and shining,
my happiness

goes on for miles
winding downtown
it leaves slivers in his hands
like fiberglass

the words don't come out in time
or they come too fast
or in the wrong order
they fly around my head in a swarm
criticism stings like a mosquito bite
the truth is a horsefly welt

love swells within me
it leaks from my pores
contentment drips down my temples like sweat
i glow and radiate

my best friend calls me her soulmate
boils me peach tea and hugs me to her chest
we fit together
with ease

it comes out of nowhere
sometimes in the earliest morning
or when everything's dark and drizzling.
echoing down every alleyway
collecting in windowsills

lonely girl

try loving yourself
as if you don't already
wrap your arms around and around
shove your own tongue down your throat
choke, leave a bruise
don't seek anything out
just lie there
let it come

look at you —
road rash and bruised shins
cubic zirconia
itchy gold and green residue
all the brown eyes that didn't teach you anything
dark hair in tangles, worn down tattoos
scythes and daisy chains
the lightsaber and the portrait of your father
the album cover a little uneven
 the scratches i left
red and raised
my gift to you

look at me
bitter and unbound

magpie

i think we never stop growing
i think we shed our previous selves
 like snakeskin,
emerge all raw and shiny
and vulnerable. endlessly becoming,
always trying to forget who we were before.

on new years eve I was in love with the whole world
inside it was warm and close
smoke curling around me, a little greasy
translucent.
i held you for a long time,
i told you a lot of things,
because my tongue was soft
and the inside of my head was floating.
we were just friends, remember?
remember the people packed into a basement, shoulder to shoulder
flowing like the changes of the tide,
a little back room, a glowing ember.
the street outside was an alien wasteland,
frozen, orange tinted
snow blew sideways
you held me in your coat
blind we stumbled
all the way down the street.
drove me home and the streets blurred to oil paint, reflecting on the concrete.
the air was so cold it hurt.

i dreamed red walls
i dreamed your hair tangling in my fingers
teeth bumping
an arm there, a leg slung over yours
i saw my body from above

when it came true
you left a bruise, delicate purple
in the corner of my mouth

so tiny you'd almost miss it.
i pressed it in the mirror
to affirm the reality,
to make sure I was awake.

you remember what i tell you.
things spoken
very quietly
in the back of a car
in the corner of a coffee shop,
the first time i fell asleep on your shoulder.
you keep memories
like a magpie collects trinkets,
you spread them out like seaglass and broken earrings
some of them shine and some of them have sharp edges.
you're the only one who remembers
you're the only one who treated me like treasure

seventeen

i never thought i'd shed my old self like snakeskin
unzip my body from within
step out
leave it like a carcass on the concrete.
emerge
shiny and vulnerable as ever.

i've never felt anything this strong and it scares me.

first summer downpour
comes and
washes away the dirt and grime
dulls the things we'd rather forget
this is a good omen.
this is a blessing
the air is heavy with humidity
i stand in front of the mirror
tilt my head to watch my skin
turn iridescent, to glow.
i turn seventeen soon
it's been four months since i first
kissed you, but
time is only what you make of it
i may be a mayfly with papery wings
i may die tomorrow.

feel the back of your neck soaked with sweat.
there are thoughts that become reality
there is a point where reality becomes undone.
curve of my thighs
dip of my collarbone
tiny birthmark tiny scar.
there are hands everywhere.
the light is a liar, plays across the angles of your face
shades of lavender
pale blue,
i tell you i like you, i do,

i like you
i am scared of the stronger word

let my mind wander
i become clairvoyant
push the years aside
like heavy curtains.
in some world
we are somewhere high above the ground.
clouds collect around our kitchen table
in our house there's
a small jungle of plants, bright screens i can't comprehend.
a clone with big brown eyes
a carbon copy with curly hair.
imagine.

imagine we left right now and never came back. imagine
the world ends
and we are buried
beneath ash and sediment.
bones jumbled so they couldn't pull us apart if they wanted to.
our bodies will fertilize what comes next.
the sun rises and
tender green shoots emerge from the earth.
i never thought it'd be you.

narcissus

i told myself it'd be different this time
wrapped my head
in cotton gauze
fixed it tightly
salted the perimeter of my room
tried to forget that i'd been warned

i could be
the turning point
the last stop

you make me
feel golden
precious like the crystals on the plants
you carefully pick from the jar
if you could be brave for me,
things would be brighter.

you were all talk,
held the sides of my face and
said things
that went through my ear and
burrowed in my brain
excuses
skittering around the corners
of my room

whatever we had,
it cracked in two
you unbutton my jeans
zipper drags
gets caught.
this is a seance,
waking something that should be dead.

your lungs are rotting
coated in soot,

19

burnt paper and grime
some essential part of me
is being whittled away
with a fruit knife,
is being served on a plate
this all
means nothing.

sometimes when you look in the mirror
i think you'll fall through the glass and drown.

clarity
you seem
a safe place to rest
but now
you're nothing tangible
i reach up to your face and
 you slip through my fingers

i see right through you
i see what you're afraid to be

first love

the mirror speaks to me
tells me I'll be okay
mirror
flushes me golden
shows me the only person who won't abandon me
no matter how hard i try to untether myself
from this body of mine

it'd be easy to pretend
i cried all night
and in the morning
you were wearing blue.
wove your fingers in mine,
it got quiet and you said
i was meant for more than this

i'm done wishing
that the world was a little brighter
and the earth spun a little faster,
wishing
that you didn't careen through life like a derailed train
blaming the tracks for not holding you down

you can share my bed still
collarbone as pillow
skin and bone
smooth me
under your thumbs.

we can play house
turn every light on
click on the stove
watch the flames glimmer blue
watch the smoke seep from my mouth

through your eyes
i was precious and

delicate as glass.
i wish you were
careful with me.

may 2018

I don't wanna forget when I was sitting on your bed and you went downstairs and brought me a plate overflowing with fruit, chopped watermelon and grapes and mango.

and when we were driving back to your house, there was a beautiful pit bull with a glossy coat hanging its head out the window of the car next to us and I wanted to take a picture so you took my phone and did it for me.

somewhere else

in another life
i step off the plane onto the tarmac
air heavy with humidity
my dress flutters,
yellow linen.

my thoughts fly wild
join the emerald parakeets
resting in the trees

he loves me
and he builds me a house
overlooking the valley
our pineapple and hibiscus
our medicine,
six feet tall with spidery thin leaves.

he wears a thin
gold chain around his neck,
veins on his hands
he sweeps me off my feet
spins me around like a doll

he works late nights
the city traps him in like a labyrinth
he grows and refines and moves and sells.
he shows it to me one day
finely milled and white as snow
pushes it around on the dining room table
trust me baby
he says
you don't want to try it.

he loves me
and he comes home
with a blazing fuschia stain on his shirt

unfamiliar perfume lingers
and stings
when he opens his mouth
centipedes slither out
pale white.
you're beautiful
he says
instead of
i'm sorry

my hair grows past my waist
diamonds sparkle from my ears
he slices mango
feeds it to me with his fingers
rub the knots from my shoulders
pulls me into bed and we sleep entangled
cicadas singing hymns from the trees

he loves me
and we die on a sunday morning in july
a storm of bullets through our front window,
they catch his chest his throat
my shoulder
my arm
between my ribs.

he clutches my arm tightly as he goes
we lay there on the carpet
pomegranate stain
wine spill
the crucifix on the wall
watches with kind eyes
the man on the cross whispers
you should have known better

our grave is granite and shining
people cry in the streets
and leave flowers on our doorstep
this is the best ending

we could have hoped for
playground

these days i try to walk only where the sun shines
the cracks in the sidewalks become canyons again
the dirt is more welcome than the pretense of being all clean, all new
in my dreams i'm never alone
i hide under playgrounds
rain soaks our clothes through
some nights
i'm sixteen again
a hand gripping my thigh in a church
while mother mary frowns down at us.
i walk other paths
shoes worn through and i turn over restlessly in bed
i am a little girl with too much time on my hands
i am more than a woman
forked tongue
many arms
some nights
you cannot contain me.

nineteen

one has been there
cobalt blue, he's been there spring green
with a soaked bandage on his face
he'sbeen there, between the hospital and the highways
i cup him in my hands
like a sweaty palmed child grasping a firefly
knowing I have to let go at some point

one burns through me like a fever
sweat soaked, endless
what he gives me is real,
tangible
i don't know when to pull the bandaid off
when cut away the rot,
but how many nights will we argue on the concrete?
drunken, reeling
tears stealing their way out the corner of my eyes
how many times will we forgive
missing
the mango nectar
honey milk
sweetness
of the familiar?

one is half memory, nothing more
some part of me rots in a landfill,
velvet plush
dirt and decay, worms all through
better not to mention
how badly i wanted
to be no longer
discarded

sore

moths to a flame
new bride
boys offering green liquid in a bottle
the third shift worker coming to free me
i am learning
that things are only scary the first time around.
see how the dust settles?
see how you'll be okay again.
i thought you were supposed to be the smart one
my friend says over FaceTime
her voice echoing in the parking garage stairwell.
i thought so too.

get home and scrub clean
the bathroom sink
soap scum
toothpaste
residue of impulsive haircuts
clean porcelain gleams up at me
like a smile

comeback

says / he wants me again / his girl looks sweet / carefully curled dark hair / a dull
kind of magic

refracted / oil and water / he asks me how his body changed / since i'd seen him last
 you're not as skinny anymore / used to be his mirror / i almost forgot / how he
used to turn / insecure / isn't that it? / porchlight / praise / warp / he shows me /
carcasses / flesh / fat sinew / the excess / he piles and packages meat / now / he's got
a mugshot too / possession / holding the block and everything / you used to / he
lays in my bed / left / doesn't lie anymore / missing / seventeen came and went /
without a word / watching / rot / slick pavement / you don't quite understand /
half stranger / first / how it feels to be discarded / gutter / landfill / rotten / how I
haven't felt anything / searing / since

j.p

paint splatter blue crust,
dishsoap
rich
layers upon
layers
of resentment
ask me a question
8 ball
a bust in a box
slide in
a quarter and
i tell a half truth
lick me clean
rub it in

why don't you
stay gone?

bad girl

bad girl
feels like she has dead flies glued to her eyelids,
their legs dipping into her corneas,
wet
porcelain doll pretty
twenty dollar bill
pressed into her hand
she has
 razor burn like a motherfucker
strawberry red pockmark
could be smoother
could
have been more gentle
some mornings
she puts on a new face,
not a mask but a veil
blue cages around the eyes
orange glow on
the cheekbones
pink — lilac
mold bloom
growing colorful

bad girl
begins again
and again

rosacea

she lives in halves and measures
ashamed to be ashamed
of the patches of pink in her cheeks
rough at the edges like a spill

that's no way to be

rapture

i stand on a wraparound porch with splintery corners / it used to be whitewashed /
eggshell dulled by dust / i clutch the porch's railing and stumble down the front
stairs / looking out over the great expanse / the clouds contorting into strange
shapes and formations / a premonition

& you called home / years ago / said not to wait up / but here i stand anyway / my
skirts blowing in the warm green wind / the promise of tornado or mushroom
cloud / irradiation / the dust storm of your car down the driveway / i brace myself
 / for whichever comes first

river

she kneels
to catch a glance
down in between the lily pads
prays to her own reflection —
who else would listen?
who else would even
know what to say?

centuries ago a girl with my face refuses to hold still.
they chisel her out of a block of red stone,
skirts flying around her ankles, forever in movement
i still hear the tinkling of bells
her screams of joy

she wades into the river
cups the water in her palms
streaming between her fingers in rivulets

sees me staring up at her

untitled

so what if the sycamore tree
doesn't blossom
the crocus hides beneath the earth, leaf brush
shrivel and blackens —

i know that won't happen and I know I have breadcrumbs down my front,
my mouth is full
i'm not avoiding you
you just make me sick to my stomach

second night with jack

i fell asleep
 on his chest
woke up at noon
drooling
on his sweatshirt
drove up
the coast
i took him to a beach
where i had gone
as a child
but when we got there
the wide stretch of sand
had been swallowed
by the tides
there was only rocks
and grassy bluff
i sat down
and got mud on my ass.

a stranger
in a fanny pack
walked up to us
and said,
"no beach?"
we shook our heads.
"no beach."

and for a minute
 i forgot
about the current state
 of things.
i drove us home
he stood
and held open the screen door
 half in, half out
kissed the top of my head
let it slam shut

i know
it'll end
like all
things do

april 2nd 2020

on valentine's day
i wore a green skintight skirt
cried in the bathroom
at the party

earlier that day
you wept on the school racetrack
before i even knew you

the red maple's blooming in erratic bursts.
my Target sandals abandoned
on the balcony all winter
i miss you
& i miss
my friends with their big incredulous laughs
and the open face of anyone willing to listen,
anybody i ever half loved
my sister running to throw her arms around my waist
it'll be over soon — right?
this will be the story
i'll tell my grandkids
how i didn't leave the house for weeks on end,
except for the grocery store,
scrubbing down the cart in alcohol wipes
imagining the festering bacteria on my hands
skin of each tomato
fell asleep at 5am
didn't cry
didn't shrivel and become small
how i sat on the balcony
the sun holding my face in her hands.

night terror

i'm only real in the sliver of the mirror
it's may and im getting my color back

i dreamt you came back and held me
we decided to try again

you breathed into my hair
sandalwood and palo santo

i said i'm scared this is a dream
you said *don't worry, this is as real*

as anything will ever be.
sometimes i can't tell, does it matter?

i dreamt i called the pretty saxophone player
from that band i like and

told him what i think,
he was hesitant on the phone.

said *i don't know you that well*
i don't know what change you'll bring.

i dreamt there was an atom bomb
dropped right in the triangle park

in our neighborhood.
i hugged my little sibling tight in my arms

as we disintegrated in a burst of white light.
but later that night

i had survived the blast, but alone
i was on a commune and the world had ended

a long long time ago

they made an apartment out of a water tower

they planted spinach and green beans
in the radiated earth, hoped

we'd get a good harvest out of it.
i was with a girl i used to like

she took me in the water tower and
let me unzip her jeans

when i kissed her i tasted her skin
i thought of it the whole next day

a spade, hands in the dirt
a water tower, her curls, her wrists

i walked around in a fog.
all this is to say

maybe someday i won't mind
how it feels to wake up alone.

repeat

10,000 of your children
sizzle in my stomach acid
sometimes when i take
it in my mouth I'm reminded
of when i almost drowned
as a kid in the five foot deep
end of the swimming pool
chlorine at the back of my throat
i like it when we lay here
the white spackle of the ceiling
like seafoam, like
scuttling clouds

keepsake

a lock on the fence in Montmartre
my name written in oil crayon on a lamppost behind the Mexican restaurant
a tape recording of my first tattoo,
in some dusty box under a bed in an attic.

the first time i slept at your house all your roommates
already knew my name
your shirt fit perfectly
and i knew where you kept your cups

how long until everyone forgets
i kept a name under my tongue
like a small stone

rajkumari

& so what
if it's been seven years
since i stepped foot
on her soil

        in the red rock palaces the doorways
        could have been carved for me

the women dancing,
carved in stone
could have been my sisters

        so what
        i eat my tamarind and green chili,
        turmeric and asefetida
        cumin and star anise
        i still eat with my hands

i still move with rhythm
bells tinkle with each step
i take

        i was born of the women
        who turned from the flames and fled,
        blackened soles

they whisper to me as i sleep
sometimes all you can save is yourself

for c.y

you haven't made me angry yet, isn't that sweet?

           i hope the first time you make me cry
              it isn't too bad

i hope our first pregnancy test
you buy me a snack, after.

             i hope you know
            i'm trying my best for you

thanks for letting me in

memorial day

the helicopters carpeted the sidewalk
like they'd fallen just for me

my therapist asks me
why i need the validation

my sandals rubbed raw spots
on the tops of my feet

my lover runs his fingers through my hair
and it feels all new

i think of the the drip castles i built on the beach
as a child

the sweet smell of lilac that my grandma
gathers for me from her garden

the purple light in my room
the pink impression left behind from tight elastic

my mom used to have a baby sister
the silk flowers on her grave
were full of ants, so we cleaned it out

for her
trowel, gloves, wire-stem peonies
wherever you are,
you you are loved so dearly

sweetie

let me peel you open like an orange
slice by slice
dig into the sweetmeat
of your belly

find glass beads and pieces of ivory
tucked between
your ribs
i kneel down and run my fingers over
your diaphragm, pet your liver
like a cat at a party

when i almost know you
i sew you back up
spit on the pink mountain range
of your stitches

you wake up with a smile
unblemished

Made in the USA
Monee, IL
16 August 2022

11792781R00026